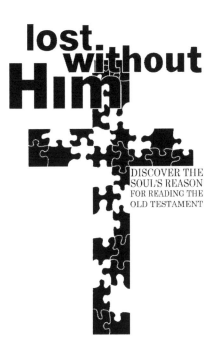

lost
without
Him

DISCOVER THE
SOUL'S REASON
FOR READING THE
OLD TESTAMENT

Lost Without Him:
Discover the soul's reason for reading the Old Testament.
My Journey Edition, January 2022
Copyright ©2012, ©2015, ©2022 by Pastor William E. Land

Book cover art: Copyright ©2012 Ben Branum
*Mount Sinai photo, (photographer unknown) is modified for color and
effect for this Personal Edition by Robert Buckner*
Original art (Page 21): Copyright ©2015 Minister Frank E. Frazier

Desktop Publishing services provided by Nekheti Nefer-Ra Edited by
Lee-Ann Stephens, Denise King
and Marilyn Parker
Book formatting by Robert Buckner

Pastor William E. Land Lost Without Him:
Discover the Soul's Reason for Reading the Old Testament
lostwithouthimbook@gmail.com
St. Albans Church of God in Christ 678 Aurora Avenue
Saint Paul, Minnesota, 55104 United States of America

ISBN: 9798402820739
Printed in the United States of America

Dedication

I dedicate this book to young minds who desire to know the truth even when it hurts at times, rather than repeating false statements as if programmed. Your quest to understand choices is essential to maintain sanity in a world where common sense is becoming increasingly blurred. And this is prevalent even in academia, where stupidity is not a lack of ability to learn; it is an education that lacks logic. It is why trusting your convictions to be and give your best is the right attitude to have when searching for the truth. "Lost Without Him" is the help you need to realize why it is God you seek. Enjoy!

TABLE OF CONTENTS

Author's Note

To those of you who are familiar with the
title of this book, I'm pretty sure you're thinking,
"Hasn't he done this several times before?" Yes,
I have; but this is a personal journey. When
the LORD led me down this road, I had never
envisioned myself writing at this level. But the
burden to do it increased. It all began around the
fall of 2011 while preparing to teach a class on
the Old Testament. Comments to write a book
on the Old Testament by two ladies, my daughter,
Adora and Sister Denise King, was like water
poured on a seed planted by the LORD in my soul
at conception. From that moment, not knowing
where this journey would take me or how long
it would last, to refuse Him was not an option I
wanted to test.

You may ask, "Was it worth it?" Of course!
Writing "Lost Without Him" has been one of the
most rewarding experiences in my life. And I
believe every attempt helped those who read the
books to realize just how priceless a jewel the Old
Testament is. Each revision had nuggets that the
one before did not have, which was a sign of my
growth during this process. If you have purchased

any book of mine on this topic, do not ever think it cost too much! Never underestimate the value of the truth in the soul of anyone who is seeking a better life.

So, you may ask, why would I want this book? My answer: It is too precious of a gem not to have for yourself. Also, because of your desire to know the truth, things you have read before will mean more, and you will see more. That's God's way of rewarding them that seek him. In addition to that, there is someone you know who needs this book. Remember, you are called to reach people where they are, not them where you are. We all have made many mistakes on this journey called life; if we have learned, it was a lesson well worth it. Please, do not hold it against me for not holding back what responsibility cannot.

And to everyone else that will read this book, **Lost Without Him** is a step-by-step approach to understanding the Old Testament. The theme throughout the book is that God loves you. How you respond to the truth will determine if you love **Him**.

Introduction

Whenever you read the Bible, it is important not to think that you can neglect certain books, assuming they are not equally as potent as other ones. As you read, you will find that the entire book is a beautiful revelation from God for everyone who seeks His love. Although there are two Testaments (the Old Testament, which consists of 39 books, and the New Testament, 27 books), make no mistake about it—the messages harmonize into one. When you read the Old Testament, think of it as a light to help us understand why we need a Savior. While in the New Testament, the Savior is the light who fulfills all of our needs.

As you read this book about the Old Testament, keep in mind genealogies, prophecies, laws, ceremonial rituals, the annihilation of entire tribes, psalms, proverbs, as well as end-time predictions are essential. Everything in the Bible is written to challenge your mind to think, hope, persevere, and trust that you will "understand it better by and by." Therefore, open your heart with anticipation and allow this book to introduce you to a fresh way of understanding the Old Testament.

Before I go into the Old Testament, I want you to think about a statement I heard my Pastor,

Superintendent Timothy L. Barge (who is at home with the LORD), say: "The Bible is like a jigsaw puzzle. Unless you know "what" the picture looks like, you will never figure out the puzzle." What he meant is, whether it is the Old or New Testament, many of the stories in the Bible require you to look elsewhere in Scripture to complete the picture. As you are looking, you will also realize that the books are not in chronological order. But even if they were, without God's help, it is impossible to know what the picture is to put the puzzle together. **Job 11:7** (New English Bible) states, "Can you fathom the mystery of God; can you fathom the perfection of the Almighty?" In other words, unless the LORD makes Himself known, no one can discern how awesome He is, or comprehend the excellent way that He exists. Neither is it possible to understand God's plan.

Therefore, when God wants to be known, it is by personal revelation and through His word. For example, when Jesus' disciples go into the world to preach the Gospel, they only have the Scriptures (the Old Testament) as the resource to affirm their message. Luke, (a believer and historian) tells us in **Luke 24:27**, which is the New Testament, why they were able to do it. "And beginning with Moses and all the prophets, He [the Lord Jesus] explained to them [His disciples] what was said in all the Scriptures concerning himself" [emphasis mine].

That confirms my point: Although they have the Old Testament, they did not understand the intent and depth of the Scriptures until Jesus took the time to explain to them all of the things concerning Himself written by the prophets—and He begins with Moses. And it will take the Holy Spirit to bring to life things in this book about the Old Testament for you to understand why God's plan is better than we can imagine.

As an outline, the first five books are called the Pentateuch or Torah. Think of them as the blueprint for the meaning of life and a guide through it. Within them are the Ten Commandments, Sacrificial Laws, and Ceremonial Laws. Following these books, from Joshua to Esther, the History books. From them, you'll learn human ingenuity does not make a person better, but having a heart for God will. Next are the Poetry books from Job to the Song of Songs (or Song of Solomon). These books are lessons about life that we should never forget. And the last thirteen are called the books of the Prophets (Isaiah to Malachi). They remind us although conditions in the world are chaotic, and death seems like an answer, life is a better choice. ***Now get ready to discover the soul's reason for reading the Old Testament.***

THE PENTATEUCH

GENESIS
EXODUS
LEVITICUS
NUMBERS
DEUTERONOMY

FAITH

The beginning: In Genesis chapters 1 and 2, we get one of those "put your explanation with your mouth" moments. What I mean is, rather than be quiet as though it does not matter, the author is challenging anyone to come up with a better explanation for the world they see. He declares: In the beginning, God created the heavens and the earth, merely by speaking the words. Then he proceeds to give some details to reveal what God did daily for six days, which was the final day of creating. On that day, God also created man, then the woman.

Furthermore, God gave creatures that fly, those in the water, things on land, as well as the man and woman, the ability to multiply or procreate. But He did not give any of them the ability to multiply outside of their kind or become something better than their created purpose. This rule also applies to insects and every other species on the earth.

However, what does not appear to produce its kind (such as water, the moon, stars, etc. is necessary for living things to survive and to fulfill God's purpose. But it is human beings that will learn in a way unlike anything else the uniqueness of created things, and their limitations.

On day seven, in Genesis chapter 1, God said that the whole universe was good and wondrous in His sight. Imagine for a moment seeing space, stars, and every planet in its totality. That is what God sees. However, if you have not heard of God, the statement "God created" makes no sense at all. And to expect anyone to believe in God without any proven knowledge is wrong. Therefore, the writer of Genesis is informing you that:

1) God has no beginning:

2) He speaks, and everything comes into existence according to His purpose; and

3) He is pleased with His creation.

These are three good reasons to consider belief in God, even if you have not heard of Him. But if this seems hard to believe, imagine nothing at all. Could anything be, including your imagination? Answer: No! That's why there is no better explanation for things created than the fact that God has always been.

Next, it is also important to believe that the earth at this time is untainted—pure of any evil. The first man (Adam) and the first woman (who later is named Eve) are the only human occupants. Question: Knowing what you see occurring on the earth today, do you think you can create a better world with people in it than this one? Some might say that's easy. **First:** We would populate the earth all at once, with only the type of people we desire to have. Every one of them would be purpose-driven. **Second:** In our world, crime or sin would not exist either, which means they cannot be tempted or distracted. And **Third:** It is a stress-free world since there is no one to worry about!

I wonder, does that world appeal to you? Let's look closer and analyze what supposedly is a better world. **First:** In that world, by creating them all at the same time, none of them are related to each other. And without family, it is an uncaring world that is absent of love. **Second:** To not be tempted "really" means they do not have free will. Therefore, such a world is also void of pleasure and hope. **And Third:** They would be right—there wouldn't be any reason to worry! All they did in that world was duplicate what they had done in this one, make things to entertain themselves. And in this purpose-driven world, did you notice the easy solution to avoid problems like today? It is not to create human beings at all!

Even though that whole scenario was imaginary, life is not a guessing game. You will never know what it means to live without the correct answer.

When God created one man and one woman, it was not to entertain Himself; neither was it a mistake. From the moment of their existence, the possibility to have the ideal experience of life and relationships is His gift to them. Also, being the only occupants on earth, all human life will be genetically connected to them. This way, there will only be one race of people—the human race. Another thing: If Adam and his wife are not aware yet, they will learn that human beings are different heights, shapes, shades, and weights, like other things they see.

Furthermore, as Adam and his wife develop, life will present opportunities for them to learn the true meaning of love and responsibility to God and each other. However, by allowing human beings to make choices, their greatest pain and joy will depend on how they choose and react to consequences. Therefore, humans are the only beings on earth that can gain or lose the favor of God with unfathomable results! *But for now, remain focused, and you will see why God never intended His plan to be a secret.*

In chapter 2, the place where Adam and his wife reside on earth is an area where they have access to eat everything that grows on the trees in the Garden of Eden, except for one tree – which means there is plenty of food to eat. However, there is no mention of them having a home. Maybe they slept on the ground or did not need to sleep at all; only God knows. But the main things that we need to know about them are written in this chapter. In it, we learn that Adam is a very intelligent man who names all the livestock, birds, and beasts of the field, and no one has more authority on earth than him. But that doesn't mean his wife lacks intelligence. God created her to be beneficial to him, as they learn the true meaning of becoming one.

Although there is not one verse in the Scriptures that lets us know how much time has elapsed, chapter 3 reveals their first challenge. And this test comes from someone they were not aware existed, especially in the manner that he appears. During this encounter, his wife is tempted and convinced that she will know as much as God, who created them.

CHOICES, PUNISHMENT & INFLUENCES

Three major events happen in chapters 3 through 11 of Genesis.

1) Sin enters the world when Adam disobeys God and eats from the only tree that is forbidden.

Immediately, they recognize the devastating consequences of their choice—shame and fear. When God created man and woman to be emotional beings, these two emotions were similar to what it would be like to be under surveillance today—but better! No matter where they are, shame and fear remind them of their obligation to God. Unfortunately, within a matter of time, attitudes that challenge His existence begin to manifest, and faith in God becomes a question mark! Unless God provides a way to redeem Adam and his wife, death will await the whole human race as an unsolvable problem.

In **Genesis 3:13-15,** a clue is given to them how He will do it, and a woman is essential for the solution. Although the lifespan of Adam and his wife (who he names Eve) will be incredibly long before physical death occurs, the harsh reality of being dead spiritually will become more disturbing. Sin will reside in the heart of every human being born of a man and a woman, giving the notion that something else is better than what God says. Some will even go as far as to believe that they are a God. It is just one of the ways that human beings will choose nonsense over their Creator.

As the population increases, the first parents (Adam and Eve) must try to cope with the unpredictable consequences of sin. Who can imagine their shock and grief when Cain (their oldest son) kills his brother Abel, the second oldest son? Then there's the uncertainty that will follow when illnesses, afflictions, addictions, and deformities gradually become a part of the human experience. It is trials like these that test a person's spirit, and out of them, they will learn what sacrifice and character mean.

In the meantime, to survive, some become skilled farmers, shepherds, builders, tent-makers, herdsmen, and makers of instruments and tools. Others will display talents, such as art, singing, or dancing. These skills and talents are keys to help them find their purpose for existing. However, it is important to know that this knowledge comes from God, who is all-knowing. Without Him, there would not be any such thing as an idea, or a reason to hope.

Now that they are becoming productive, the challenge is to love one another—this will not be easy. Sin is creeping into their homes in various ways, arousing the emotion of dishonesty, anger, hatred, jealousy, pride, greed, rebellion, vengeance, lust, laziness, or self-centeredness. Unless they humble themselves before God, it will be difficult for them to love each other because trust and unity will fade. (Note: When you read chapters 3 through 11 of Genesis, although there are not a lot of rules forbidding the behavior I've mentioned, their conscience is alerting them that these things are wrong.)

As family life becomes more and more challenging, sin is getting increasingly worse, especially for those who are ignoring their conscience to justify sinful behavior. In contrast, others believe the conscience is necessary to steer them in the right direction for a better life. Enoch is one of them. Known for his walk with God, when he vanishes suddenly for his commitment to God, his family continues to warn the world for generations of their disobedience to the LORD. Unfortunately, their success seems minimal due to so many rejecting what the messengers of God have to say.

2) Hundreds of years after Adam's death at nine hundred and thirty years old, a great flood covers the whole earth.

Sin has twisted the minds of the people to believe that God's existence and His judgments are nothing more than lies and threats. Thus, God punishes them severely to enforce the fact that faith in Him matters. Only a man named Noah, his wife, their three sons (Shem, Ham, and Japheth), and their wives find favor with God and survive the flood, as well as selected species and animals, by being inside an ark.

After the flood, two very important things happen.

First: Noah builds an altar to make sacrifices to God as an expression of thanks for His mercy. By shedding the blood of certain animals and birds, Noah is acknowledging that there is both forgiveness of sins and salvation with God.

Second: God makes a covenant with them and every living thing, never to destroy the entire earth with water again. Immediately, the sky becomes radiant with many colors that bend like an arch from one side of the earth to the other. From this moment on, this will be a sign whenever it is seen, especially to the human race, that the word of the LORD will stand forever. I should also mention that the lifespan of everyone born will be drastically less than their ancestors—while sin will seem like it is just getting started.

3) Generations later, the people go from one universal language to confusing languages.

No longer can bullies (such as Nimrod) or manipulators control large groups of people as they once did. Changing the language makes them sound stupid! God did this to humiliate the arrogant and to give hope to the weak-minded. As the people begin to split up and associate with the ones they understand, family traditions, cultures, and beliefs also change. **The search for good leaders begins.**

WHO'S LISTENING?

From chapter 12 through chapter 21 verse 7 of Genesis, a 75-year-old man named Abram hears the voice of God telling him to leave his relatives and country. The LORD promises Abram that through his seed all nations will be blessed. So, Abram did as the LORD said; he departs his country Haran with his wife (Sarai). But for some reason, he did not leave behind his nephew Lot. Unaware of the trials ahead, Abram reserves time (at certain destinations) to acknowledge God and to call upon Him for counsel.

So far, the LORD's promise to Abram that through his seed all nations will be blessed has not happened. What they may not know, there is more to this promise than they think. Unless their firstborn is a male, it will never happen. Although they have tried to have children, their attempts have been unsuccessful because Sarai cannot get pregnant. Subsequently, being without children, and an attractive woman for her age, will leave Sarai vulnerable when Abram encounters a situation that will test their faith.

As they journey south in the land of Canaan to find water and grass for their flocks and herds, Abram and Sarai discover when they get to their destination that the land is not suitable for their livestock. Famine has spread throughout the land. Thus, Abram decides to leave the land of Canaan to go down to Egypt. As they get closer to Egypt, fear causes Abram to convince his wife Sarai to say (if questioned by the Egyptians) she is his sister. If God does not intervene on their behalf, this could turn into a nightmare or shameful experience for them. Fortunately for these two, He does; and they leave Egypt without losing their dignity. Not only is Abram very wealthy, but all the people with him also go with their possessions.

However, some time afterward, a dispute arises between the men who worked for Lot and those that are loyal to Abram, causing them to separate from each other. Lot chooses Jordan, where he thinks is the best land, leaving the land of Canaan as the only option for Abram to reside. But challenges cannot prevent God's plan for Abram and Sarai. Later on, Abram receives an unexpected blessing from the king of Salem, whose name is Melchizedek. His life is a foreshadowing for Someone that is the source of all blessings.

But when you think Abram and Sarai's trials are over, time reveals something else. Abram, who is now 86 years old, fathers a son named Ishmael, whose mother is Hagar. Although Sarai wanted her husband to have a child, the reality of it is more than she anticipated; and this trial will take some time to resolve. Thank God, within four years He renames Abram, Abraham; and Sarai, Sarah. It is a reminder that He will not waiver on His covenant with them or their offspring. Sometime after this, God tells Abraham what to do with his son and the boy's mother.

As they await the fulfillment of God's promise, other issues arise. Later, Abraham pleads with God to spare the city of Sodom if there are fifty righteous people in the city; but they were not there. He then reduces that number five more times, eventually hoping that God will spare the city if there are ten righteous people in it—but he could not find them either. However, since Abraham's nephew Lot lives in Sodom with his wife and two daughters, God provides a way for them to escape, if they heed His instructions. Subsequently, only three of them get out of Sodom alive to talk about it—Lot and his two daughters.

However, Lot's wife sees leaving Sodom differently. The choice she makes reveals there is something about that place that she will miss. When God's judgment falls on Sodom and the city of Gomorrah due to their wickedness, He also punishes her for disregarding His instructions about Sodom. Instantly, she becomes a pillar of salt. Afterward, whenever the topic of Lot's wife comes up, she is remembered as the woman who chose doom over opportunity.

As time passes, Abraham and Sarah end up in

another situation like the one they experienced in Egypt due to Abraham's lack of truthfulness. This time it is in Gerar, and the king's name is Abimelech. **(Genesis chapter 26.)**

God, who is faithful, comes to their rescue again and delivers them. Within one year, the LORD fulfills the promise He made to them: Sarah gets pregnant (at the age of 90) and gives birth to her only son Isaac. And her husband Abraham is 100 years old. One day he will be called the father of God's chosen people—and Sarah will be a symbol of freedom.

As you continue through the Old Testament, one of the challenges you may face is genealogies, especially if you are unfamiliar with the names. To get the most out of them, the book of Genesis mainly focuses on Abraham's lineage, especially his son Isaac. Isaac's willingness to trust his father unconditionally when it could have cost his life is a clue to understanding how God will redeem His people. You should also pay attention to Isaac's son Jacob, whom God renames Israel, which means the one "who wrestled with God" to win His favor. By studying Jacob's lineage, you will see how God's plan to redeem the human race will come through this bloodline of Abraham and not his son Ishmael.

From Jacob, there are twelve sons, which make up twelve tribes. (Genesis chapters 29-30, and 35.) Together they are known as the children of Israel, or

Israelites. Years later, Jacob's descendants will also be called Hebrews, Jews, or Jewish people. Through his lineage, the children of Israel will reign as an example to other nations. However, the fulfillment of that promise to the children of Israel/Jewish people will not happen until Someone from the ancestral line of Judah comes and takes what is rightfully His.

In the meantime, there are trials ahead that the children of Israel must face. The LORD told Jacob's grandfather Abraham, 89 years before his death at the age of 175 years old, his descendants are going to become slaves for 400 years in a land where they do not belong. However, before this prophecy, God promised Abraham that his seed would inherit a certain portion of land to occupy for many generations. Although that has not happened, it doesn't seem possible that the children of Israel could become enslaved either, especially since they are doing very well for themselves. Nevertheless, the children of Israel do end up in slavery.

If you study the life of Jacob in Genesis chapters 25, verse 20 through chapter 49, there are valuable lessons to learn about favoritism, deception, love, reconciliation, grief, reunions, and peace. These are serious topics that every person should be acquainted with, especially if they desire to have a healthy family and relationships.

When Jacob turns 147, He dies in the land where

his descendants will become slaves. After Jacob's son Joseph, his brothers, and all that entire generation dies, the influence that the children of Israel have in Egypt will begin to diminish. Soon a king rises and plots to deal with them deceitfully. Hence, Israel will experience bondage—a hardship previously unknown to them.

During this time, the children of Israel's loyalty to God and each other faces several tests. The horror of being in bondage for almost 320 years (so far) can break the spirit of anyone who feels inferior and hopeless. Those that yield to temptations to impress their oppressors do not mind betraying family members for personal benefits, while others abandon their teachings to fit in by adapting to the Egyptians' ways. Although these details are not in these books, their attitude to question and disobey God is the root of that behavior. Thank God, some would rather endure harsh treatment meant to break them than to compromise their faith in Him. I tell you, God will not forget them; and many will witness what seemed to others to be a dream!

What is interesting, despite their unpleasant conditions, the children of Israel are having babies at a rate that far exceeds their oppressors. In Egypt, the place of their bondage, Pharaoh (the king), fearing the possibility of being overthrown, is determined to weaken the children of Israel for generations to come—and no age is off-limits to his cruelty. Compared to today, Pharaoh was not confused about his decision. When Pharaoh ordered to have all baby boys that are three and under killed, even he knew the only either/or in a woman's womb is a boy or a girl. And he did not pretend that it wasn't murder. Nevertheless, a Hebrew baby is found by the banks of the Nile in a basket, who will one day be known as a deliverer. And it is Pharaoh's daughter who named him Moses, which means taken out of the water.

From his childhood, Moses grows up in the house of Pharaoh, who is clueless about Moses' heredity and calling. But Moses learned a lot about the Egyptians' culture and the Jews. When he is 40 years old, Moses goes out one day to evaluate the labor done by the Hebrew people when he sees one of the Egyptian men beating a Hebrew man. Upset by his behavior, Moses has an altercation with this man and kills him. Once Pharaoh finds out, he intends to kill Moses. For this reason, Moses flees Egypt and goes into the land of Midian, a place that he is not familiar with at all.

While in Midian, Moses meets and marries his wife Zipporah and starts a family. As Moses adjusts to life as a shepherd there, Pharaoh dies in Egypt. However, the children of Israel continue to cry out to God for help due to being oppressed by another Pharaoh. During this time, Moses is unknowingly being prepared by God to lead them out of Egypt.

After being in Midian for 40 years, Moses (who is around 80 years old) is out attending the flock when he comes to the mountain of Horeb. While he is there, he has an encounter with God on this mountain.

The LORD speaks to Moses from a flaming bush that he notices is not being consumed. His message, I am the God of Abraham, Isaac, and Jacob, who hears the cries of the children of Israel due to their oppressors. Then God informs Moses, I have chosen you to lead them out of bondage. From this moment, Moses must learn what it means to walk by faith. Unaware of the magnitude of this task, he asks God, "Who should I say sent me?" And the LORD says: "Tell them I AM THAT I AM sent you." It signifies that He is the eternal God who is complete within Himself.

To reassure Moses that He is the Creator of all things, the LORD displays more of His power to him. However, that does not completely relieve Moses from the heavy burden he feels to lead the children of Israel out of Egypt. For this reason, the LORD provides Moses with inside support from family members and others to help prepare the children of Israel for their exodus from bondage. Nevertheless, it is Moses who will tell Pharaoh (the Egyptian king) that the LORD said: "Let My people go!"

When Moses confronts Pharaoh in Egypt, the

LORD works mighty wonders through his life. Nine plagues fall upon Pharaoh and his people; still, Pharaoh refuses to let the children of Israel go. Appearing unshaken by the plagues, unknowingly, the final plague will hit Pharaoh and the Egyptians where it will hurt the most—and that is in their hearts. They will learn within twenty-four hours that Passover is more than a Jewish ritual.

On the day of Passover, the children of Israel kill the firstborn male lambs (without defects) that are a year old. Blood from the lambs is put on both sides and across the top of the door-frames of their homes. During the evening, a special meal is prepared for them to eat. Around midnight, while the children of Israel and others celebrate Passover, death passes over them—and every living thing necessary for their survival. However, for Pharaoh and the Egyptians, death enters their homes as a plague!

As the day continues, the children of Israel can taste victory, while Pharaoh and his followers smell death. Imagine for a moment the firstborn of everyone you know, and every firstborn animal, all dying on the same day. This is what happens to Pharaoh and the Egyptians. Although the death of their livestock and servants is an incredible loss to them, they never anticipated dealing with the grief of losing their firstborn sons, or the children of Israel's exodus from Egypt. Devastated by the final plague, the Egyptians willingly give them whatever they ask for as about 600,000 men depart Egypt on foot. Also, all of the women, children, and the rest of the men leave Egypt, as well as others who were not Israelites. (**Exodus 12:31-38.**)

However, the children of Israel are not free from Pharaoh until the LORD parts the Red Sea, which they cross over it on dry land. But that did not frighten Pharaoh from sending his army to go after the children of Israel. As his army attempts to cross the Red Sea on dry land, the waters cover them. Results: They all drown! The children of Israel are ecstatic, and they celebrate their freedom by giving thanks to God for His mighty power on the day of Passover. To them, their four hundred years of bondage are over. And for generations to come, other nations will hear about this day, which will be called one of the greatest defeats of all time.

Remember these words: A celebration is only a shallow expression of joy masking the fear of what lies ahead, while joy is the highest form of celebration in the face of that which is considered frightening.

Do you know crossing the Red Sea does not mean that they are free to live by their own rules? Soon God will reveal to Moses a system specifically designed for someone to make intercession before Him on Israel's behalf. This system is called the

Priesthood, and the place is the Tabernacle or the Tent of Meeting.

Although the threat of Pharaoh is behind the children of Israel, their journey to reach the Promised Land will not be easy. After leaving Egypt, while in the desert on Mount Sinai (or Horeb), Moses seeks direction from the LORD away from the people. When he returns to them, the elders and the people agree to adhere to the word of the LORD. Soon after this meeting, Moses goes back to the LORD with their commitment to obey Him. During this time, the LORD establishes a covenant with the children of Israel on two tablets of stone.

Would you believe it's only been three months since Israel's exodus from Egypt, and the people grow suspicious of Moses when he does not return as soon as they thought—even though he had taken this trip before and returned? It is sad! Once the seed of doubt is in the minds of the children of Israel, they question the leadership of Moses and God, who delivered them out of the hands of Pharaoh. Before the children of Israel know it, the majority of them are worshiping an object made by their own hands—instead of the Creator who gave them hands.

God, fully aware of their activity, admonishes Moses to return to the people. After witnessing their blatant disrespect for God, Moses is outraged.

So, he breaks the tablets that would bring the children of Israel into a better relationship with the LORD. Repentance will spare most of them, while punishment for the rest is fatal.

Eventually, the children of Israel receive the written law given to Moses from God, which is called the Ten Commandments. These laws will give them a new identity as His chosen people. Written within the Commandments are instructions on how to worship Him as the only true God. Included are rules to live morally amongst each other by respecting the laws that discipline bad behavior. There are also dietary laws, dress codes, and ceremonial cleansings, as well as rituals for justification, atonement, sanctification, and glorification. Besides that, the LORD even sanctions a specific day (called the Sabbath) for them to rest every week. The meaning of that day will have eternal significance for everyone who believes in Him.

However, these ceremonial cleansings and rituals are not sufficient to wash the children of Israel thoroughly from their sins because they are constantly repeating them. A reminder that the stronghold of sin requires more to eradicate it. And because of their unbelief, many of them are dying in the wilderness. Nevertheless, God continues to make provisions for the children of Israel for years as they travel to get to the Promised Land. Whether it is Manna (food) from Heaven, their clothing, a pillar of fire by night, or a pillar of cloud during the day, there are many valuable lessons to learn from their experience—and patience is one of them. Also, the Tabernacle is a reminder of God's "Holiness" and their responsibility to strive to live holy by obeying Him.

Original Art by Minister Frank E. Frazier

(If you want to learn more, study "the Tabernacle" and "the Ark of the Covenant.")

For now, to continue to have God's favor upon their lives, sacrificing certain animals is required to cover Israel's sins and prevent His wrath toward them. The stipulation is that the offering must also be a firstborn male without defects or blemishes. Whoever performs these ceremonial cleansings and rituals must be declared holy to fulfill their duties unto God as a mediator for His people. **(To learn more, read the book of Leviticus.)** Even though that person is incapable of living a sinless life, neither are firstborn animals nor any other morally perfect; the LORD still requires this sacrificial system to be done. Although these observances may not make sense right now, hopefully, you will appreciate them. Within this sacrificial system is God's plan to "eternally" redeem the human race that's lost without Him.

As you follow the children of Israel's path closely, the Savior will come like a seed that sprouts in its season. He will handle the word with a skill that only God could have. His message will soothe and convict the souls of the multitudes that follow Him. Prophesied, even before His birth, Someone will shed their blood and become the perfect sacrifice by fulfilling God's promise—to Israel first, then to the rest of the world—for forgiveness and redemption. Like a shepherd who protects his flock, He will secure the hope of everyone who believes in Him when He solves the problem of death by overcoming it. This Person is the Savior of the world.

As they continue on their journey, God's choice of Moses to lead the children of Israel out of Egypt and through the wilderness reveals how much He loves them. Under the leadership of Moses, other nations feared the children of Israel because of the LORD's favor upon him. Through Moses, the LORD demonstrated signs and wonders never seen before. Many of that day said that Moses' had a face-to-face relationship with God. After wandering in the wilderness for a total of forty years, Moses dies at the age of 120 years old—the children born in the wilderness grieve over the man many of their parents and grandparents had frequently opposed. *(Read the book of Numbers and Deuteronomy to gain a better perspective of the trials Moses had to face in the wilderness.)*

HISTORY BOOKS

JOSHUA

JUDGES

RUTH

I SAMUEL

II SAMUEL

I KINGS

II KINGS

I CHRONICLES

II CHRONICLES

EZRA

NEHEMIAH

ESTHER

COMMITMENT, CHALLENGES & COURAGE

To grasp the magnitude of the wilderness experience, if you estimate the number of people that left Egypt (**Exodus 12:31-38**), you can assume it was at least three million people. What is interesting, out of those who were over twenty years old, only three see the Promised Land. They are Moses, Joshua, and Caleb. But it is Joshua and Caleb that (actually) enter the land. God rewarded their unwavering faith to trust in Him even when it wasn't popular.

As the children of Israel move forward, God will destroy the obstacles in their way. Under the leadership of Joshua (Moses' successor), most of the children of Israel are enjoying the most prosperous and peaceful time of their history because the LORD fulfilled every promise to them concerning the land they occupy. After Joshua's death (110 years old), Israel continues to reap the benefits of peace and prosperity for serving God. (**Joshua chapters 23-24.**) If you can recall what I said in the Choices, Punishments, and Influences section, there is a clue on page sixteen and the reason for their success. Answer: It is because they used the talents and skills given to them by God to become one for His glory. **That is the key to life.**

Although this is called the history section, the

first five books are also reliable historically. To become a better student of the word (when you study this section), list the leaders you admire for their commitment and courage—leaders such as judges, priests, prophets, and kings. Study their faith, doubts, fears, and arrogance as well. As you identify with specific individuals, you will learn why humiliation is the only way for a man like Samson to see his need for God. Also, for those of you who believe in male dominance, there are some extraordinary women in the history books as well. However, you will have to judge for yourselves. And if you enjoy a love story, the book of Ruth is for you. It will make you think, what is love without a kinsman-redeemer? Learning who that represents in the fullest sense is very important for their salvation—and ours.

However, as a warning, there are places within the history books when God's judgments may appear too harsh the first time you read them. Here are two examples: At certain times during a war, God commands the leaders of Israel to kill all of their enemies, including the children. A command is also given for leaders of Israel to kill some of their relatives and the children also. Perhaps to you, taking the lives of children you deem innocent is unjust. However, God is the only one that can authorize the taking of lives without minimizing their relevance for being. By

sanctioning their deaths, maybe God spares them
from a judgment far worse due to the influence of
their wicked parents.

As an alternative, you can choose not to believe
in God at all. But how will you cope with the
problem of losing a loved one if their life is taken
unjustly without becoming insensitive, numb, or
hopeless, especially if death is the end? Think about
it: Human justice can only release, punish, or kill
the perpetrators. But the death of the murderer
cannot equal the life of a loved one to a grieving
family. Neither is it of any benefit to the victims
whose lives have vanished. And if the fate of every
person who dies is extinction, to say any life is
better than another is only an expression for the
living because the dead surely would not hear that
"compliment." As you can see, when a person denies
the existence of God, they have chosen to believe
that justice for all does not matter.

However, when it comes to our God, who is
eternal, He has a purpose for every life conceived.
He knows the intentions of their heart and
the potential that each person is capable of in
this world. Therefore, never think that because
someone's life is cut short due to a criminal act or
misfortune, it has somehow robbed them of life.
Although they are absent from us, thank God, He
gave us the ability to store precious memories of
them in our minds. But more than that, we can

also find comfort in knowing they will never be out of His presence since God is everywhere. And because He is all-powerful, when God speaks to the dead, they will get up and listen!

I suggest that you pray for more understanding and faith to trust the LORD, who is Sovereign, to show eternal grace to the faithful and eternal justice to those who deserve punishment. Trust me when I say, no other belief in the world answers these tough questions like the Bible.

Listen carefully, as you read a statement I made earlier in this book. It reads: Humanity's greatest pain and joy will depend on how we choose and react to consequences. Know this: The choices we make and our reaction to the consequences due to a choice someone else made will determine whether we are overcoming life's challenges with the truth, or the challenges of life are overwhelming us for denying it.

Notice when you read First & Second Samuel and First & Second Kings, how Israel is like one huge roller coaster—up one moment and down the next. They always seem to be one thought away from something destructive. In First Samuel, the children of Israel have a leader who cares about them, yet the majority of them desire someone else. Wanting so much to be like other nations that have a king, they request to have one themselves.

Although the LORD, through His messenger, (Samuel), gives detailed reasons why a king is not good for them, the children of Israel still prefer to have a ruler over them. Since they cannot be persuaded to change their minds, the LORD allows the children of Israel to have a king—his name is Saul, and they are excited!

As the years' pass, so does their excitement. Israel's king sees an enemy named Goliath that he cannot conquer, and they are terrified! Right when you think the children of Israel are doomed to destruction, God, who is merciful, sends a small solution for their giant task. To their surprise, a shepherd boy, who seems unequipped to fight the enemy, will defeat him. He will become one of the greatest warriors of his time and the next king of Israel—his name is David. As the king, the LORD establishes a covenant with David that his kingdom will never end. To learn a lot about his character, read First Samuel chapter 16 through First Kings chapter 1, verse 13. From these scriptures, you will learn how David's poor choices had tragic effects on his family.

As you read more about David, you'll also notice how his faith in God helps him face complex issues. People will call him "a man after God's own heart." Before his demise, God honors the covenant with David, and his son Solomon succeeds him as the king over Israel. He will be famous around the world for his wisdom, wealth, and for building the temple. It is another step in the plan of God that will eventually lead to the revelation of the KING of kings.

By the time the fourth king is appointed, a rivalry ensues that splits the tribes, producing two kings and kingdoms. Judah is the southern kingdom, whose king is Rehoboam. And Israel is the northern kingdom, represented by Jeroboam. Both have their issues. The things that God warned the children of Israel about concerning a king are coming to pass, and it is haunting them. Whether it is the southern or northern kingdom, when Israel excepted a king, they forfeited their rights to remove him. From now on, the king in charge, his family, or whoever overthrew him will determine the next ruler—unless the LORD intervenes on their behalf.

As the kings change, the children of Israel do not know if they are getting a good or bad king. Some start well, but as time goes on, many of these kings become more and more corrupt. Consequently, the northern and the southern kingdoms will reap the effects of their bad behavior. The children of Israel will either end up exiled from their land or are like strangers in it because their cities are left in ruins. Furthermore, even the most sacred things to the children of Israel's faith and worship are also taken or destroyed. All of this is because the majority of them make an emotional decision that the rest have to learn how to overcome.

Does this sound familiar to you? Think about it: The pain and suffering that continues throughout this world today is mainly the result of decisions made in the past to ignore warnings. By thinking they knew what was best for them at that time, they placed their hope in the idea that evidence is wrong. Thank God, He continues to raise men and women who weigh the facts, not their feelings, before making decisions. Therefore, when called upon, they know how to deal with or fix problems that others find overwhelming.

Another example of this in the Old Testament is the story of Esther. It is the last book in the history section. In the book of Esther, she must personally weigh the cost for the true meaning of life and pleasure. To some, that might seem like an easy answer, especially if they knew Esther lives in a palace. But that doesn't mean she has a carefree life. You see, Esther must decide if it is better to remain silent to maintain her lifestyle of wealth and fame or risk losing it for listening to her cousin Mordecai. His message (to her) is that Jewish people (their relatives) will hang if she doesn't speak up. Question: What would your conscience have to say about that if it were you? It's a classic lesson on what is more valuable—wealth and fame or faith. And whether you admit it or not, the way you live reveals what you value most. *(To learn more about the Jewish people, read I & II Chronicles, Ezra, and Nehemiah.)*

POETRY

JOB
PSALMS
PROVERBS
ECCLESIASTES
SONG OF SONGS*

*(ALSO CALLED THE SONG OF SOLOMON)

INSPIRATION, WORSHIP, WISDOM & LOVE

What does it take to inspire hope within you? You've read quite a bit about the pitfalls of life when someone rebels against God. Likewise, what those who did not compromise achieved. Although you can learn from a bad example what not to do, good examples tend to raise our expectations faster and higher. Another example of one having strong faith in God is Job. Maybe his trials, mixed with tragedies, while questioning his existence, are the stories you need to read.

In the book of Job, he will hear from people close to him, telling him how to treat his pain or the reason for it. His wife said, (paraphrased) "If you want your pain to go away, denounce God and die!" But his friends said, "Job, this is a judgment upon you. Why won't you just admit you did something wrong?" As you go through this book, certain events will cause you to question God's character. On the other hand, you can learn from Job what it truly means to trust in God, even when human reasoning or feelings suggest something else.

Take, for example, if you're wondering why bad things happen to good people, the book of Job addresses this very well. When you read it, remember this: If it is wrong to test good people with bad things, then what standard was used to determine them as being good? Keep in mind: Since good is the opposite of evil, to be good, you must know better and do better. Job is proof that the best thing a human being can do is to put their faith in God or collapse under adversity.

Next, pay close attention when you read Psalms. It begins by describing the man as blessed who does not walk in agreement with ungodly people. Neither does he stand attentively to take the advice of sinners to keep him on the right path. He never sits in their company listening to derogatory jokes about God or His people. His time is much too precious to spend hearing miserable men *(whose lives are a pitiful expression of potential)* mocking God and others to avoid the pain of seeing themselves. This man, who is blessed, finds utter enjoyment in the law of the LORD; and his life inspires hope in others that there is a better way to live.

However, the way for the sinner is much different. It is a common theme for a life without God, where the naive are bound feeling hopelessness due to their inability to recognize deception. And those who happily spread deceit are bound due to their distorted definition of hope—unaware that they will not escape God's judgment.

Without a doubt, you do not want to neglect reading the book of Psalms. I can truly say, no matter what your circumstances may be in life, there are statements or prayers in this book to lift your spirit. If you feel shame or guilt, read about the agony of King David, as well as others who cried out to God to forgive their sins. Discover how liberating confessing your sins are when you desire true happiness. Not only this, there are prayers to God to vindicate you from your enemies as well. You know who I am talking about—those people that intentionally try to sabotage your life or do things to hurt you. If this is your dilemma, learn from the psalms how to trust in God to deal with them.

From the book of Psalms, you will also learn how to reverence God, who is Holy and Sovereign—even when you're all alone. When you need guidance, during the lows, or highs of life, the psalmist calls Him the only Shepherd you want. The more you read, the more you will learn that Psalms is about having a personal relationship with the LORD. Within the message of these writers, you can sense that it is important to them to have God's mercy and His righteousness. It is the only way to fill the emptiness inside. You see, in the psalms, the Messiah is not only the fulfillment of Israel's desire for mercy and righteousness—He is ours as well.

For this reason, certain clues are given in the psalms to help the children of Israel to identify the Messiah when He enters the world. As things unfold in His life, the statements he will make during His most trying times will take away every reason the Children of Israel think they have not to believe in Him.

But before I finish this section on the Psalms, you will never know the value of it unless you learn from it the importance of patience, humility, the statutes (laws and decrees) of the LORD, songs of praise, and a place to worship. Believe me: you will need each one to be a light for others to believe your relationship with God is real. To read the Old Testament without Psalms is like having the best lyrics without the melody to set the mood. My advice to you, surrender to His plan and be taught by our omniscient God, or your life will be a proverb on foolishness.

Now, to avoid having an out-of-control life, ask God for knowledge and understanding. The appropriate use of these two together makes a person wise, which is the highest honor of credibility obtainable for human beings. When acquired, men are known for being trustworthy and women for being virtuous. So, when "Mr. Trustworthy" and "Miss Virtuous" meet and marry, they understand that truth is the foundation for love, and accountability is the reason for submission. When they have children, their relationship with God will enable them to discern the children's differences as they grow up. This way, each child can get the nurturing they need from parents who exemplify what it means to live for God. ***Can you imagine the success rate for parenting if every Christian took this approach to raise their children?***

Also, to those who are single, Proverbs is the book for you. At the core of it is a deep concern for our state of mind. This book reminds the reader that God is the epitome of knowledge, understanding, and wisdom. These three must be your most treasured companions; otherwise, you are not ready to withstand the temptation of loneliness, drinking, finances, and eating. To pursue happiness without God's principles to govern your heart will only amount to an endless cycle of disappointments.

Next, if that did not inspire you to get closer to God, read about Solomon, the king of Israel, in Jerusalem. He thinks his wisdom allows him to indulge in worldly pleasures and avoid the consequences by outsmarting them. From these writings, you will learn that temptation does not discriminate against anyone. Neither is folly limited to a specific class of people. Therefore, never make the mistake of revering anyone because of their wealth, talent, or education. Life under the sun is not about pursuing personal dreams to prove one person is superior to another. The human experience is much more complicated than that.

Trying to figure it out on your own is impossible; it is like chasing after the wind. In this book, the king eventually admits that the only reasonable conclusion to draw from life is no one deserves worship except God. Govern your life by His word – you will be glad you did! On the Day of Judgment, God will examine everything you have done. **That is the book of Ecclesiastes.**

The last poetry book addresses a topic many think is taboo in the Bible—intimacy. In the romance between a man and a woman, the lover and his beloved, it is clear that God has uniquely designed us to have a special relationship with the opposite sex. That is why there is not one verse in the Bible that mentions intimacy like this with the same gender. When you read this book, notice how possessive the man and the woman are of each other. Then pay attention to the descriptive language used to visualize the other's body. Notice their desire to be one—body, soul, and spirit. Now before you allow that uncontrollable emotion called lust to overtake you, hear the repeated warnings not to awaken love until the proper time. Hidden within this dialogue is the Savior's love for His bride. *I suggest, do not omit reading any of the Poetry books!*

REFLECTIONS & LOOKING FORWARD

After learning about various topics in the Bible, take a little time to process this information, especially if you were unfamiliar with the Old Testament. In what ways has this book been beneficial for you? Now select a particular topic and write a paragraph about it in your own words. Think about God's plan for the human race and how the children of Israel were used to spread His message. Hopefully, this will prevent you from making the same mistake many have, underestimating what God wants them to know. Keep in mind; I've only given you highlights from the books I've addressed so far in the Old Testament. There are so many more life lessons in them that are just as interesting and insightful, but that's someone else's responsibility.

Up to this point, you have briefly covered 22 books in the Old Testament. There are only 17 left—Isaiah to Malachi. Before I move to the Prophets, did you notice that freedom does not necessarily mean a person has peace? Israel is an excellent example of this. No matter where the children of Israel were, whether leaving Egypt or entering the Promised Land, they were still searching for it. Their rebellion against God caused many of them to overlook the place where peace is needed the most—the heart! However, some did demonstrate great faith and courage to trust God's plan for their lives. His word gave them hope, while His promise gave them peace. *I hope this reading has given you more confidence to trust His promises.*

Now that you have gone over the Pentateuch, history, and poetry books, keep in mind the Scriptures are not always in chronological order. For example, the book of Job is the oldest in the Old Testament by most scholars—even though it is eighteenth in order, starting with Genesis. In the books of the Prophets, do not be surprised that their ministries overlap. What I mean is, some of them are prophesying concurrently. And some prophecies are given as if they have already happened. The best way to explain this is these prophets had to believe their predictions came from God. To make such statements for any other reason would be detrimental to them. Under the Mosaic Law, the penalty for making false prophecies is death!

Also, if you desire to increase your understanding of the Old Testament, I want to encourage you to purchase a Bible concordance and study Bible. In addition to that, a Bible commentary is also essential to have. When researching a particular subject in the Scriptures, you will find these books very helpful. Just make sure your study Bible or Bible commentary has maps and charts to trace the children of Israel's journey. They are necessary (if interested) to have an idea of the dates these events occurred.

As you enter the final books of the Old Testament, called the Prophets, I pray, this section will give you a deeper appreciation for the inspiration of Scripture. Without God's promises and the prophetic word, there is no reason to expect anything from Him. ***Let's see if God fulfills His word. If so, pray for an ear to hear what the Spirit is saying to you. Then ask God for the Spirit of obedience***

THE PROPHETS

ISAIAH

JEREMIAH

LAMENTATIONS

EZEKIEL

DANIEL

HOSEA

JOEL

AMOS

OBADIAH

JONAH

MICAH

NAHUM

HABAKKUK

ZEPHANIAH

HAGGAI

ZECHARIAH

MALACHI

DECLARATION, REJECTION & HOPE

In the last 17 books of the Old Testament, the LORD assigns prophets to declare His word to the northern and southern kingdom. Earlier, when the kingdoms split, the calamity that followed caused the children of Israel to be in different areas. Therefore, prophets are called by God at particular times, for particular groups. From the prophets, God's chosen people hear frequent messages to repent and believe his ultimate plan for humanity. Other nations also hear but ignore God's warnings, so He punishes many of them severely. However, although Israel (the northern kingdom) and Judah (the southern kingdom) are just as guilty, the LORD does not renege on the promises He made to the children of Israel. (Note: That does not mean God is soft on judging them. No one gets away with sinning. The penalty for sin will happen when it's least expected. And it will be worse than imaginable for those who find pleasure in sinning.)

In the book of Jeremiah, the prophet tells a king named Jehoiakim that none of his lineages will ever reign as king over God's people. Even though God punishes him severely, this seems to contradict God's covenant with his ancestors—Abraham, Isaac, Jacob (also called Israel), Judah, and king

David. That Someone from their ancestral line
will reign forever as the KING of kings. Unless a
miracle happens, one cancels the other. Still, it is
God's people who held on to His promises and died
believing that the Messiah would come and fulfill
them. Thank God, it was the blessing of assurance in
His word! In Isaiah, the Messiah is God our Savior.
In Jeremiah, He is the LORD our Righteousness.
In Daniel, the Messiah is the Ancient of Days,
and in the book of Zechariah, He is the Almighty
King, while in Malachi, He is the Messenger of the
Covenant.

Unfortunately, many of the children of Israel are
still deaf to the prophetic word. You wonder, what
will it take for them to believe? When you read the
books of the Prophets, you might be surprised that
God's chosen people (the children of Israel) are
prostituting themselves, behaving like whores; yet
even that is not enough to shame many of them
to repent. In the book of Hosea, believe it or not, a
prophet marries a prostitute—even though he is the
messenger against immorality. That man is Hosea.
But if you think he is unfit to be a voice against sin,
you may think differently after reading the book.

Elsewhere, in the book of Ezekiel, a story is told
about some dry bones scattered over a valley. The
LORD asks Ezekiel, "Can these bones live?" Once
you realize the bones represent the children of

Israel, you might think, why should I care? Well, one day you are going to be a pile of bones!

Also, in other books, certain things sound fictitious.

Here are just two examples in the Old Testament:

1) In the book of Daniel, three young men are thrown into a fiery furnace and don't get burned; and

2) in the book of Jonah, he is swallowed by a big fish and lives to tell of this experience.

What is unexplainable to us, such as miracles, can only happen because of God. He can do anything—as long as it does not conflict with His character. For example, God cannot be an enemy to Himself, which means, He cannot create a situation impossible for Him to handle. Neither can beings He created with free will cause a problem He cannot solve or cure. That's why misfortune is not a legitimate excuse to justify failing, nor is it a good reason not to become a better you.

When you read the books of the Prophets, Israel's behavior will affect you differently. Amos, at times, wants justice to roll like a river upon the children of Israel because of their foolish behavior. Jeremiah pleads in his soul to God, who is merciful, not to consume them because of their addiction to sinning. Then there is the disappointment Hosea felt after learning these people are perishing due to a lack of knowledge—because they reject knowledge. I must say, it is "very" easy to be critical of the children of Israel until certain behaviors seem familiar to you. That's when the personal revelation comes: I am or was just like them, a slave to sin.

Thank God, Someone was wounded for the transgressions of the whole world and bruised for all of its iniquities! The LORD has placed upon Him the burden due to our sins. To His delight, this Person needed to suffer severely and die. Because failure was not an option for Him, He perfectly made intercession before God on behalf of sinful humanity (Isaiah chapter 53). Therefore, people everywhere will have the opportunity to know the true meaning of love and responsibility. To seal these promises, the prophet Joel said (Joel 2:28)," The LORD will pour out his Spirit on all flesh." But that does not mean all who live their lives trying to find fulfillment in it.

I can tell you this, of all the literature that you can read, no other book prepares you for the challenges life brings better than the Old Testament. It is the soul's reason for reading it. As a believer, I thank God for the men and women, from Adam and Eve to the Prophets, who withstood the pressure of the world because they trusted their convictions. Although they were not fortunate to witness the fulfillment of their prophecies at that time, the mission to prepare the way for the LORD continued.

PROMISE KEPT

To the children of Israel and all who believe that the promised seed of Abraham has come, rejoice! As it is written in **Isaiah 9:6**, "For to us a child is born, to us, a Son is given." Do you remember this statement? "The Bible is like a jigsaw puzzle. Unless you know "what" the picture looks like, you will never figure out the puzzle." Well, the picture is of Jesus, the only Son of God.

In the first book and chapter in the New Testament, which is Matthew, the genealogy of Abraham is on display as validation of the Old Testament account. From his son Isaac and many generations afterward to king David, hundreds of years more to Joseph, fate becomes a reality. The angel of the Lord appears to Joseph in a dream and tells him to marry a young lady who is a virgin. Her name is Mary (also of the ancestral line of king David, **Luke 3:23-24**), but she is also pregnant. What may seem absurd to some is a miracle to others when she has her first child—a Son. And the expectations are high for Him to be the Redeemer of the human race. His name is Jesus. The Shepherd that leads humanity in the way of righteousness and peace. Every problem known to the human experience, whether physical, emotional, mental, or spiritual, is solvable. But not for those who refuse to put their faith in Him; these are benefits they would lose.

When Jesus died on the cross for the sins of the world, truth and consequences meet. Buried shortly afterward as the only sinless sacrifice, He rises from the dead on the third day. The ceremonial cleansings and rituals, including the sacrifices of animals once required, are no longer necessary for the children of Israel that placed their hope in Him. Now, His righteousness covers them as a garment to shield them forever and everyone else that believes in Him. Hear the words of Jesus, the Messiah. "This is what I told you (His disciples) while I was still with you: Everything must be fulfilled that is written about me in the law of Moses, the Prophets, and the Psalms." "Afterward, He is taken up into Heaven." (**Luke 24:44- 51**, New Testament book.)

Brothers and sisters, if you avoid studying the Old Testament, it is impossible to appreciate the New Testament. For without the Old Testament, thinking the New Testament is sufficient is to expect people to believe it is possible to have power without a source.

I hope the information in this book has given you the spark needed to pursue a deeper relationship with God through the Scriptures. If so, as your passion increases for God, so should your desire to reach souls *lost without Him. It is the only way to improve the world we see and have a life that continues to improve beyond this one.*

God bless you; I love you in Christ.

Pastor William Land

Biblical References

Afterword

Do you remember this statement? A celebration is only a shallow expression of joy masking the fear of what lies ahead, while joy is the highest form of celebration in the face of that which is considered frightening. By observing the children of Israel, you must conclude: The majority of them went through life pretending to have a good time with no regard for the consequences, while the rest found true happiness in the LORD's plan despite adverse conditions.

I firmly believe that there is no better explanation for our existence or solution for sinful behavior than the story you have just read. Also, did you notice, there was no mention of the devil's power? That is because the power of God transcends all that evil can be. Therefore, you are without an excuse.

Acknowledgments

Seldom do we realize the impact others have had on our lives when our paths crossed. Most times it is not until later in life that we become aware that they were God sent. And since so many have encouraged me in my walk with the Lord, it would be impossible for me to name them all. I only know their labor was not in vain in the Lord. However, I would like to acknowledge two men that helped me more than they could ever know. They are Bob Karklin (who went home to be with the Lord), and Gerald R. Johnson. I met them while working at Honeywell International, Inc., years ago. Their friendship and generosity toward me transcended the bias often seen in some who profess Christ. For this reason, they will always have a special place in my heart.

Also, in memory of my most treasured friend and pastor, Supt Timothy L. Barge Sr., who is at home with the Lord. His obedience to the call of God helped me to realize there is no better choice in life than to serve the Lord. I had never heard anyone preach about Christ the way he did.

To my wife, Shirley: Your commitment to the Lord is a testimony to many why God ordained marriage. He knew I needed you in my life. I love you for loving me to stay true to who I am in Christ Jesus.

To Travale and Quanita, TaDarrean, Adora and D'Sean, William II, and Destyn: Thank you for being there whenever I needed you.

To all of my brothers and sisters, in-laws, my Aunt/Mother Willie Flower, cousins, nieces, nephews, and grandchildren, Khamani, Kobe, and Mattiyahu: Much love to all of you from me.

To all my friends from Mt. Airy Projects, Mechanic Arts High School, Honeywell, and elsewhere: I thank God we crossed each other's path.

Special thanks to Bishop Fred Willis Washington of the Church of God in Christ, Minnesota Jurisdiction (COGIC), for the opportunity to teach a class entitled, Old Testament Survey.

Very special thanks to Sister Denise King. God knew I needed your assistance when I first started on this road to writing Lost Without Him. And He knew it would not end without you. Thank you for sharing your precious gift to understand the English language. God Bless you!

And to Bob Buckner: The sacrifices you have made and creative insight were indeed a blessing. But even more, I thank God for our friendship.

Likewise, to Minister Terry Stephens and the Stephens family, you will always be in the hearts of the Land family.

Finally, to three of the most influential ladies, I have ever known—my mother, Elnora Land, my godmother, Effie Clemons, and my aunt, Mother Ernestine Pruitt. Also, to the best male role model I knew growing up, Uncle Booker T. Pruitt. Thank God, they have ceased from their labor in the Lord and have entered into His rest.

About the Author

My husband, William Earl Land, Sr, is the Pastor of the St. Albans Church of God in Christ in Saint Paul, Minnesota, where he first started attending around 16 or 17 years old. His mother, Elnora Land, exemplified how one should live as a Christian, and her influence and many others were instrumental in shaping his life. When he was younger, he had a Sunday school teacher named Mother Mary Rhodes (now at home with the LORD) who told him, "God would give him wisdom." And from the moment William gave his life to Christ, he seemed to have an intense desire to know the word of God. After he became a Pastor in 1997, his sermons were heard (for two years) on a radio program called 'Crumbs from the Master's Table Ministries,' which he founded. But it was after a stroke in 2009 his passion for writing a book started. And if you knew my husband, you would understand why he continued to revise his books. It is not for money! He refuses to quit if he believes it didn't meet God's standard for that assignment. And if you have been on this journey as our family has, you may be saying, when does it end? I can tell you this; there is no better way to complete the task given to him by God. Whether it is his book "The Trinity: A balanced message for level-headed people, or Lost Without Him: Discover the soul's reason for reading the Old Testament, "My Journey" best describes his desire to know and share what is true.

William is a man of God who loves the Lord. His life has been an example to me, our sons, our daughter, and many more that he has encountered. I hope his journey has made yours a lot easier.

Shirley B. Land

Made in the USA
Middletown, DE
28 October 2022